The Africans

Jen Green

CRABTREE
Publishing Company

PMB 16A 350 Fifth Avenue
Suite 3308
New York, NY 10118

612 Welland Avenue
St. Catharines, Ontario
Canada L2M 5V6

Co-ordinating editor: Ellen Rodger
Content Editor: Virginia Mainprize
Production Co-ordinator: Rosie Gowsell
Cover design: Robert MacGregor

Film: Embassy Graphics

Printer: Worzalla Publishing Company

Created by:
Brown Partworks Ltd
Commissioning editor: Anne O'Daly
Project editor: Caroline Beattie
Picture researcher: Adrian Bentley
Editorial assistant: Chris Wiegand
Maps: Mark Walker
Consultant: Professor Donald Avery

CATALOGING-IN-PUBLICATION DATA
Green, Jen.
    The Africans / Jen Green.–1st ed.
        p.cm.– (We Came to North America)
    Includes index.
    Summary: Recounts how Africans were originally
brought to North America as slaves and how they
eventually flourished in the face of overwhelming
prejudice.
    ISBN 0-7787-0184-0 (RLB) – ISBN 0-7787-0198-0 (paper)
    1. Afro-Americans–History–Juvenile literature. 2. Slavery–
United States–History–Juvenile literature. [1. Afro-
Americans–History. 2. Slavery–History.] I. Title. II. Series.
    E185.G755 2000
    973'.0496073–dc21   LC 99-085754
                            CIP

Photographs
Brown Partworks Library of Congress 15
(bottom), 18 (top); National Archives 5
(top); **Corbis** 17 (top), 19, 21 (bottom);
Adam Woolfitt 4; Bob Krist 26; Bojan
Brecelj (title page), 10; Buddy Mays 28; J.
Sohm/ChromoSohm (front cover),
27 (bottom); Jacques M. Chenet 31
(bottom); Neal Preston 30 (bottom); Owen
Franken 5 (bottom); **E.T. Archive** National
Maritime Museum 13; **Hulton Getty** 22
(bottom); **Image Bank** Archive Photos 16
(top), 23 (top), 24, 29 (top right), 30 (top);
Image Select 23 (bottom); **Nova Scotia
Archives** Bob Brooks Collection 25 (top);
Peter Newark's Pictures 9, 11, 14, 15
(top), 16 (bottom), 17 (bottom), 18
(bottom), 20 (top), 20 (bottom), 21 (top),
25 (bottom), 29 (top left), 29 (bottom
right), (back cover); **Robert Hunt Library**
22 (topa; **Werner Forman Archive** British
Museum 6, 7 (bottom right); Entwistle
Gallery 7 (bottom left).

Cover: Family members sing gospel at a
family reunion in Washington, D.C.

Book Credits
p. 8: *A Narrative of the Life and
Adventures of Venture, a Native of Africa
but Resident about Sixty Years in the
United States of America*, published in
New London, 1798.

page 12: *The Interesting Narrative of
the Life of Olaudah Equiano or
Gustavus Vasa, The African*, published
in New York, 1791.

Contents

Introduction

The first Africans came to North America with Spanish explorers almost 500 years ago. Together they opened up the land to European settlers. Within 100 years of their arrival however, Africans were bought and sold like animals and became the personal property of white masters. Unlike other **immigrants** who arrived with hopes of a better life, they had been kidnapped from their homelands in Africa, chained together, and shipped across the Atlantic Ocean to become slaves.

For hundreds of years, the history of Africans in North America has been a brave struggle against harsh treatment, unfair laws, **prejudice**, and **racism**. They have had to fight hard for their freedoms and for equal treatment.

Sold into slavery

Millions of African slaves were brought to North America from the 1600s to the early 1800s. Most were sent to work as laborers on the **plantations** in the south and the West Indies. Others became household slaves in the eastern and northern United States. In the French **colonies,** later known as Canada, there were some slaves, most of whom worked as personal servants. Slaves had no rights. They, their families, and all they owned, belonged to their white owners.

Some white people never approved of slavery. They thought it was wrong for a person to own another human being. During the late 1700s, more and more people became aware of the evils of slavery. They began to support the **abolitionist movement**, which worked for equal rights for all people. One by one, the countries of Europe that had been most involved in the slave trade passed laws to stop the buying and selling of slaves.

▲ When African men and women were caught as slaves, they were chained and marched to the coast to be sold to slave traders. The larger ring was put round their neck, and one smaller ring was put round each of their wrist

By the 1820s, slavery had also ended in the northern United States, but the southern states were determined to keep slaves. It took a terrible conflict, the American Civil War (1861–1865), finally to end slavery in the United States.

Even after the end of slavery, blacks in the United States and Canada still suffered many years of prejudice and **discrimination**. In some areas, blacks were **segregated** in schools, churches, and public places. So, they set up their own schools, churches, and community groups. These organizations worked hard to fight discrimination and win equal rights for all black people.

▲ In the 1950s, African Americans held public protests to end unequal treatment.

▼ Today, in the United States and Canada, black and white children attend the same schools.

Equal rights

During the 1950s, African-American leaders increased their public protest against unfair treatment. They led marches and gave speeches. They organized demonstrations to force the government to pass laws giving equal rights to all people. By the 1980s, the last racist laws in the United States had been abolished. Despite the changes, black people still have to work for equal treatment, fighting racism wherever it occurs.

A Proud Heritage

White slave traders and slave owners did not believe that slavery was wrong. They thought that whites were superior to blacks. Yet, for thousands of years, Africa was the home of many ancient and great civilizations.

Most of the Africans who were kidnapped and sold into slavery came from West Africa. For hundreds of years, West Africa had been a vast region of rich and powerful kingdoms. The first of these great **empires** was Ghana, which arose around 700 A.D. It was a wealthy and powerful country because it had a vast supply of gold. The king had an army of 200,000 men. His court was magnificent, and he was waited on by an honor guard carrying golden shields.

Nine hundred years ago, the kingdom of Mali became the most powerful empire in Africa. Mali was a center of trade and learning. Under Mansa Musa, the greatest of all its emperors, Mali became the second largest empire in the world at the time.

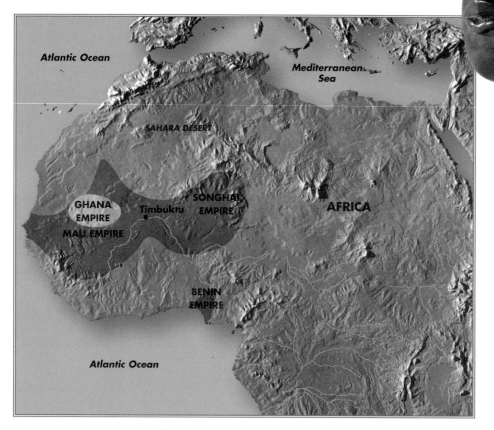

▲ Idia, the mother of a West African king, lived in the sixteenth century. The cap that covers her tall hairstyle is made of coral beads.

◄ This map of North and West Africa shows the empires of Ghana, Mali, and Songhai, in the 1400s.

The Origins of the Slave Trade

For thousands of years, people all over the world have kept slaves. For example, slavery existed in Greek city states, the Roman Empire, and in Africa, where, at first, most slaves were prizes of war — men, women, and children captured by victorious armies. The arrival of the European traders in Africa led to a trade in slaves on a much larger scale. French, English, Portuguese, and Spanish explorers had reached North and South America and were setting up colonies in the new world. Large numbers of workers were needed in the tobacco, sugar, and cotton plantations of the West Indies and American colonies. From the late 1500s, European slave traders began to ship Africans to the Americas. Within a hundred years, the slave trade was booming.

By the 1400s, when the first Portuguese explorers and traders arrived in West Africa, the Songhai empire under its great king Askia Mohammed Askia was the most powerful. Songhai covered much of West Africa. Askia's rule was a time of **prosperity** and peace. The famous city of Timbuktu became one of the most important trading centers in the world. Endless **caravans** of merchants came from distant lands, crossing the Sahara Desert on their camels to exchange their wares for gold. Metal workers, potters, and weavers made tools, weapons, beautiful statues, and finely woven cloth.

Scholars from Europe and Asia came to Timbuktu to study at its famous university. The city was home to some of the greatest **astronomers**, **mathematicians**, and doctors of the time.

▼ A sixteenth-century mask made for a West African king. Carvings of Portuguese merchants' heads decorate the top.

◄ This brass plaque, which shows two Portuguese traders, decorated an African king's palace. The Portuguese first came to Africa to trade gold with the Mali empire.

Eyewitness to History

Broteer, the son of a West African prince, was kidnapped from his home by slave traders when he was eight years old. He was marched to the sea where he was taken onto a ship and sold to his new owner for four gallons of rum and a bit of calico cloth. Broteer was renamed Venture Smith, arrived in North America in 1737, became a slave, and later dictated his story, *A Narrative of the Life and Adventures of Venture, a Native of Africa.* Here, he describes how he was captured and sold into slavery.

" The very first salute I had from them was a violent blow on the back part of the head with the fore part of a gun.... I then had a rope put about my neck, as had all the women in the thicket with me, and was immediately led to my father, who was likewise pinioned and haltered for leading.

The invaders then pinioned the prisoners of all ages and sexes indiscriminately, took their flocks and all their effects, and moved on their way towards the sea.... All of us were then put into the castle, and kept for market.... I and the other prisoners were put on board a canoe, under our master, and rowed away to a vessel.... While we were going to the vessel, our master told us all to appear to the best possible advantage for sale. I was bought on board by one Robertson Mumford, the steward of said vessel, for four gallons of rum, and a piece of calico, and called "Venture," on account of his having purchased me with his own private venture. "

Journey into Slavery

From the early 1600s, for over 200 years, African men, women, and children were sold into slavery and shipped across the Atlantic Ocean. Many died before they reached North America.

The new colonies in North America desperately needed workers, especially the southern plantations. Soon, the slave trade became a fast-growing and **profitable** business. In Africa, local chiefs were encouraged by European traders to capture or kidnap entire villages of other Africans and sell them as slaves. Men, women, and children were caught, herded like cattle, and chained together to stop them from escaping. They were forced to march to the coast where the slave ships waited. Thousands of Africans died of hunger and cruel treatment along the way.

On the coast, families were split up and regrouped according to age, sex, and fitness. Merchants inspected each prisoner carefully, since only strong, fit workers and healthy children were worth buying. Those people thought to be unhealthy were killed or left to die far from their homes.

▲ Four African women stand chained together at a slave-trading center in Africa.

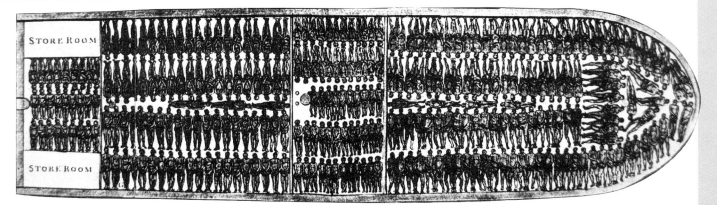

The journey across the Atlantic Ocean took seven weeks in good weather, longer if there were storms. The slaves were herded into the dark dungeons in the ship's **hold**. Hundreds of prisoners were packed below deck like animals. They were given little food, few clothes, and were often beaten. Male slaves had iron chains around their ankles and wrists and were chained to their neighbor. They were allowed on deck for only a few minutes each day. Women and children were also locked in cramped quarters but were not chained because they were less likely to revolt. In these filthy conditions, disease spread, and many slaves died.

Some prisoners tried to kill themselves by refusing to eat; others tried to jump overboard. Some slaves rebelled against their captors, but most slave rebellions were put down brutally. In 1838, on the Spanish ship *Amistad*, Africans captured as slaves revolted and forced the ship back towards Africa. They were recaptured but eventually set free and allowed to return home.

▲ **This plan shows how a slave ship was designed to hold as many African men and women as possible.**

The Triangular Trade

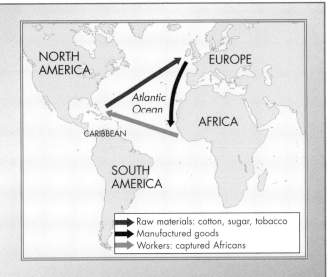

The African slave trade was part of a larger trading system between Europe, Africa, and North America. It was called the triangular trade because it involved three voyages. The first part was called the Outward Passage. Ships sailed from Europe to Africa with a **cargo** of guns, alcohol, and metal goods. In West Africa, these products were exchanged for slaves. On the Middle Passage between Africa and North America, the ships carried slaves. In North America, the slaves were traded for sugar, rum, tobacco, and cotton, to be shipped on the Inward Passage back to Europe. Merchants made huge profits from this trade in human cargo.

Eyewitness to History

OLAUDAH EQUIANO was born in 1745 in Benin, West Africa. When he was eleven, he and his sister were kidnapped from their home while the rest of the villagers were working in the fields. He was sold into slavery. After having been a slave for most of his life, he was given his freedom. Here, he tells about his voyage across the Atlantic on a slave ship.

" Under the decks...I received such a salutation in my nostrils, as I have never experienced in my life: so that with the loathsomeness of the stench...I became so sick and low that I was not able to eat, nor had I the least desire to taste any thing. I now wished for the last friend, Death, to relieve me; but soon, to my grief, two of the white men offered me eatables, and on my refusing to eat...flogged me severely.

The stench of the hold while we were on the coast was so intolerably loathsome, that it was dangerous to remain there for any time, and some of us had been permitted to stay on the deck for the fresh air; but now that the whole ship's cargo were confined together, it became absolutely pestilential. The closeness of the place, and the heat of the climate, added to the number on the ship, which was so crowded that each had scarcely room to turn himself, almost suffocated us. This produced copious perspirations, so that the air soon became unfit for respiration, from a variety of loathsome smells, and brought on a sickness among the slaves, of which many died.... This wretched situation was again aggravated by the galling of the chains, now become insupportable.... The shrieks of the women, and the groans of the dying, rendered the whole a scene of horror almost inconceivable. "

First Impressions

By the 1600s, slavery had been introduced in the British, French, and Spanish colonies in North America. In ports all along the east coast, slave markets were set up for the buying and selling of slaves as they came off the ships from Africa.

After their long and terrible journey, many slaves arrived sick and weak. The traders wanted them to look as fit as possible so that they would fetch a good price at the slave auctions. As the ships neared land, the traders prepared their human cargo for sale. Slaves were forced to wash and rub palm oil on their skin until it gleamed. The men were ordered to shave. The gray hair of older men and women was dyed black so that they looked younger. Signs of illness were also hidden.

For Africans, the first impression of North America was terrifying. The cities were strange and filled with oddly dressed white people who did not speak their language. The new arrivals were herded off the ship and displayed for sale. Slaves were examined like animals. Buyers poked their bodies, checking for strength and fitness. To judge their age and estimate how many years a slave could work, buyers forced the Africans' mouths open and checked their teeth.

▶ **This poster shows that buying and selling people as slaves was quite common during the middle of the nineteenth century.**

$1200 TO 1250 DOLLARS FOR NEGROES

THE undersigned wishes to purchase a large lot of NEGR[O] for the New Orleans market. I will pay $1200 to $1250 [for] No. 1 young men, and $850 to $1000 for No. 1 young wo[men] in fact I will pay more for likely

NEGROES

Than any other trader in Kentucky. My office is adjoi[ning] the Broadway Hotel, on Broadway, Lexington, Ky., where my Agent can always be found.

WM. F. TALBOT

Humans for Sale

There were two kinds of slave sales: public auctions and scrambles. At auctions, slaves were often placed on a high platform so dealers and plantation owners could see them and make bids. Each slave went to the highest bidder. The dealers did not care whether friends or families were divided. Scrambles were even worse. They took place in a crowded hall or on board ship. First, a general price for the slaves was settled. Then, at a signal, the buyers rushed among them and simply grabbed the men and women who looked the fittest.

▶ **At this auction, a mother and daughter cling together before being sold to different masters.**

The viewing was followed by the bidding and buying. Families and friends were split up, never to see each other again. After being bought, slaves were often given new names and sometimes branded with a burning iron to show who their owner was.

Traders unable to sell all their slaves would simply go to the next port, and try their luck at another auction. They thought of their slaves as property, or things to be sold for as much money as possible.

▼ **Two female slaves being branded with an iron that has been heated in the coals in the brazier on the ground.**

A Life of Slavery

Most Africans were sent to work as field slaves on plantations in the southern United States. Others worked as house slaves and personal servants.

On the sugar, cotton, and tobacco plantations of the south, slaves worked from dawn to sunset. White masters were rarely seen in the fields. To control their slaves, they hired harsh and cruel managers, or overseers. These men whipped slaves, who often died from their injuries.

Field slaves usually lived in run-down shacks. They were given little to eat and no medical care. Many slaves died young. The conditions for house slaves were a little better. Women worked in the kitchen, cleaned, sewed, and looked after their master's children. Men worked in the house or as grooms, blacksmiths, weavers, carpenters, and shoemakers. House slaves were better fed and clothed and were more likely to be freed than those working in the fields. Because their owners always feared they would revolt or escape, slaves were not allowed to learn to read or write.

In the northern states, farms were small. Farmers owned only a few slaves and often worked side by side with them. In northern towns, house slaves had a little more freedom than in the south. Because their masters' houses were small, slaves lived separately in slave districts.

▲ Picking cotton by hand was back-breaking work. Here, a plantation manager weighs baskets of cotton.

▶ Slaves cut down sugar cane, watched by a slave-driver with a whip.

Freed Slaves

Not all Africans in North America were slaves. Some were freed by their masters when they became too old or sick to work, or as a reward for some special act of loyalty. Others were able to buy their own freedom, called a "manumission," by saving up money earned through skilled work over many years. By the 1800s, communities of freed slaves had grown up in many parts of North America. Freed Africans still suffered prejudice and discrimination and could only take low-paid work.

▲ **Although some slaves were given, or bought, their freedom, they still worked hard and lived in poverty.**

Through all this brutality, slaves found ways to **resist.** They participated in work slowdowns, **arsons,** and sometimes tried to escape. Slaves were punished severely for such acts. Sometimes the only way they could resist was to sing work songs in the fields or keep their true thoughts to themselves. One old slave song tells of this silent resistance: "Got one mind for the boss to see...got another mind for what I know is me."

▼ **Slave children worked as servants in the houses of the rich.**

Slaves as Property

Slaves were the property of their masters. They earned no wages for their work and were ruled by strict laws that gave them no rights. Slaves who committed minor offenses were beaten or whipped; those found guilty of serious "crimes," such as leaving their master's land without permission, could be killed or tortured. Slaves were often forbidden to marry. Children born to slaves were also slaves; they were given light work at around the age of four and then full-time work by the age of fourteen.

Protests against Slavery

By the late 1700s, more and more people felt that keeping human beings as slaves was wrong. A movement to abolish slavery began. Many people, black and white, risked their lives to free slaves.

In colonial America, many people wanted freedom from British rule. Some felt that they could not expect freedom for themselves if they did not give freedom to everyone living in the colonies, including slaves. The movement to free slaves grew during the American Revolution of 1775–1783.

During this war, many slaves left their masters. Some fought with the colonists for independence. Others fought on the side of the British, who promised them freedom. At the end of the war, some of these slaves went north to Canada. They settled in Nova Scotia, which was still a British colony.

▲ This poster warned escaped slaves that police officers and others were allowed to kidnap them.

◄ Thousands of slaves fleeing from their owners made their way to freedom in Canada.

Runaways and Rebels

In the south, slaves continued to suffer harsh conditions. Many ran away from the plantations and tried to reach the north and particularly Canada, where runaways lived in freedom from the 1790s. The Underground Railroad was the name given to a secret network of people and **safe houses** that helped fugitive slaves escape to freedom. During the early 1800s, thousands of slaves fled from the south. Many were guided by "conductors," brave former slaves and whites opposed to slavery. Harriet Tubman was a guide who made the dangerous trip nineteen times, helping over 300 slaves to freedom. She brought escaped slaves to St. Catharines, Ontario. Other railway stops, or terminuses, where escaped slaves started settlements, included Amherstberg, Ontario, across the river from Detroit, Michigan, and Chatham, Ontario.

Some slaves tried to seize their freedom by rebelling against their masters. In 1831, Nat Turner, a runaway slave from Virginia, who believed he was called by God to free all slaves, led a unsuccessful revolt. With five others, he massacred 60 whites on nearby plantations, throwing the entire south into panic. Nat and his followers escaped and hid in caves but were tracked down and hanged.

▲ **The Underground Railroad led slaves to freedom across Canada and the United States.**

The war ended in victory for the American colonies. Because of opposition from the southern states, which relied so heavily on slave labor, the new constitution did not abolish slavery. It declared that the slave trade would end by 1808. Large numbers of Africans were brought into the United States just before the deadline. Even afterwards, slaves were smuggled in illegally. During the 1800s, the slavery issue divided the northern and southern United States. One by one, the northern states abolished slavery, but the south was determined to keep it.

▶ **Harriet Tubman was an escaped slave who helped hundreds of other slaves flee to the north on the Underground Railroad.**

Abolition and Reconstruction

By the 1830s, slavery had been abolished throughout the British Empire, including Canada. In the northern United States, all slaves had been freed. Only the southern states held onto the old system.

In the United States and Canada, black leaders such as Sojourner Truth, Harriet Tubman, and Frederick Douglass, all of whom had been slaves, called for abolition. So did a growing number of white people. The American author Harriet Beecher Stowe's novel *Uncle Tom's Cabin*, published in the 1850s, described the hardships of plantation life and told of slaves escaping to Canada. The book became very popular and helped convince thousands of white people that slavery was wrong. The story was based loosely on the life of Josiah Henson, who escaped to Dresden, Ontario, and later founded a community for ex-slaves.

As the movement to end slavery grew in Europe, Canada, and the northern United States, the south became more determined to keep slavery. In 1860, Abraham Lincoln, a member of the new Republican Party, a political party opposed to slavery, was elected president of the United States.

▲ In the United States, most of the north was against slavery, while most of the south supported it.

▶ In 1869, the 15th Amendment gave voting rights to *all* male U.S. citizens.

Even before he was sworn into office, seven southern states **seceded** from the Union to form their own government, called the Confederacy. Four other states followed. When Confederate soldiers fired on Union troops on April 21, 1861, the Civil War began. It was the bloodiest war in U.S. history.

Thousands of African-American soldiers fought for the Union during the four years of bitter fighting. Many former slaves living in Canada returned to the United States to join the Union army. The Civil War ended in 1865 with the defeat of the south. Slavery was finally abolished in the United States.

▲ These soldiers are on the Union side in the American Civil War of 1861–1865.

Reconstruction

The American Civil War left the south in ruins. Newly freed African Americans had no role in the new system. From 1865 to 1877, the **reconstruction** program helped to set them on their feet. The Freedmen's Bureau set up schools and colleges, and helped freed slaves to buy land and find work. New laws gave African-Americans more rights. In 1866, the 14th Amendment gave citizenship and equal rights to all people born in the United States. In 1869, the 15th Amendment gave African-American men the vote. Several ex-slaves

▲ The students and teachers who studied and taught at a Freedmen's school in South Carolina.

went on to become congressmen or governors. Despite the new laws, African Americans still experienced hostility, particularly in the south. During the late 1800s, southern states introduced Black Codes. These laws limited the rights of African Americans and denied them the vote. It soon became clear that those people who had supported slavery did not want to change their old ideas and ways.

Eyes on the Prize

Although slavery was forever abolished in the United States in 1865, true equality for African Americans and African Canadians was still a long way off.

In the south, freed African Americans still suffered from hostility, discrimination, and unequal laws. During the late 1800s, the southern states imposed Black Codes that denied African Americans basic rights. Laws were passed that all voters had to pay a tax and pass a **literacy** test. Because most former slaves did not know how to read and write and had very little money, they could not vote. In some areas, **curfew**s forced African Americans off the streets after sundown. They could not hold a meeting unless a white was present. Societies such as the Ku Klux Klan in their white, hooded robes, terrorized African Americans, burning their homes, beating them, and even murdering them.

▲ Although slavery was abolished, many African Americans still lived in poverty.

▶ African-American and African-Canadian soldiers served their countries in World War I (1914–1918) and World War II (1939–1945).

Progress at Last

During the early 1950s, discrimination was still widespread in the south with "whites only" signs common in many public places. In the mid-1950s, African-American leaders found new ways of fighting for their rights. In 1955, protesters in Montgomery, Alabama, **boycotted** city buses after Rosa Parks, an African-American woman, was arrested for refusing to give up her bus seat to a white man. The movement was led by Dr. Martin Luther King, Jr., a Baptist minister who believed in non-violent protest. After this successful campaign, Africans throughout North America began to use boycotts and demonstrations to fight racist laws.

▲ Africans were not allowed in many places.

▼ Long after slavery, many black people were still used as cheap labor for picking cotton.

African Americans who stayed in the south had little money and no land. Driven by hunger, most were forced to work as **sharecroppers** for white landowners, laboring long hours in exchange for a share of the crop they grew. Looking for work and a better life, many thousands of African Americans moved to the cities in the north. They were paid less than white workers for the same labor and were given the hardest jobs. Cheap black labor was considered a threat, and African Americans could not join workers' unions.

During World War I (1914–1918), more blacks moved to the cities with the hope of getting work. Many companies refused to hire black workers even though jobs were left empty by soldiers who had gone to fight in the war. At the end of the war, black workers were often fired so white ex-soldiers could get their jobs back. Other blacks in both the U.S. and Canada joined the armed forces. They returned home often to find no work at all.

Organizations, such as the National Association for the Advancement of Colored People (NAACP) and the National Urban League, were formed to fight unequal treatment and laws. These organizations worked to end discrimination, but real equality was still only a dream.

The Fight Continues

Thousands of African-American and African-Canadian men and women served their countries during World War II (1939–1945). Although they fought bravely, they often returned home to find prejudice and, in many places, discrimination and hostility.

In the 1950s, most schools in the southern states did not admit African Americans. They still lived in segregated areas, were allowed only upstairs in theaters, and were forced to sit in certain areas on buses. They were confined to blacks-only sections of restaurants and could drink from blacks-only water fountains. African-American leaders decided the time had come to protest publicly against this discrimination.

The civil rights movement began as a series of non-violent protests and demonstrations against unfair treatment of African Americans. In 1955, Rosa Parks refused to give up her bus seat to a white man and was arrested in Montgomery, Alabama. Dr. Martin Luther King, Jr. and Ralph Abernathy formed the Montgomery Improvement Association to show support for her. African Americans boycotted the city's buses until the U.S. Supreme Court ended special seating in 1956. Demonstrations continued across the south. Some civil rights leaders were beaten up and even killed. They were jailed, their houses were bombed, their families threatened. Still, they continued the fight.

"I Have a Dream..."

In 1963, Dr. Martin Luther King, Jr. led a march of 210,000 demonstrators to Washington to mark the 100th anniversary of the abolition of slavery. At the Lincoln Memorial, he made his famous speech containing these words, "I have a dream...that we will be free one day." Dr. King dreamed that one day black and white children would live and play together without fear and racism.

Dr. King continued the fight for freedom until he was **assassinated** in 1968. Other leaders carried on his work after his death.

▲ Brave African Americans, such as Dr. Martin Luther King, Jr. fought for freedom and justice.

Tearing down a Town

While the civil rights movement was fighting for equal rights and opportunities through the 1960s, city council in Halifax, Nova Scotia, approved a plan to tear down an all-black community called Africville, on the outskirts of the city. Black people had lived in Nova Scotia since arriving as British **Loyalists** during the American Revolution (1775–1783). Africville was a settlement established by former slaves who came to Canada after the war of 1812. It was a symbol of their freedom. Residents owned their own land and built houses and businesses in the community. In Africville, they could escape the racism they experienced in the city. However, residents were never given water, sewage, or electricity, despite paying taxes. The city council also built a prison and a sewage plant on the edge of Africville.

▲ **Africville before it was torn down. The town site is now a park.**

Finally, from 1964 to 1969, the city bulldozed the community because it was thought to be ugly. Residents opposed the destruction but were told it was not their decision. Africville was gone, and its residents lost their sense of community.

In the 1960s, the U.S. government passed laws officially ending segregation in public places. The U.S. Congress outlawed the literacy tests and taxes that had prevented many African Americans from voting. They had gained equal rights in the eyes of the law, but many continued to live in poverty in inner-city neighborhoods. African Americans continued to experience prejudice in society. Some angry and frustrated African Americans joined groups such as the Black Panthers and the Black Muslims. Leaders, such as Malcolm X and Eldridge Cleaver, who had little faith in the government and the police, called for blacks to take control of their own communities. They organized projects, such as free breakfasts for disadvantaged children and free health clinics in inner-city neighborhoods across the United States. Black power leaders encouraged black people to start their own businesses and told them they could be proud of their history and achievements as North Americans.

▲ **This 1960s poster shows the salute and the slogan of the Black Panthers.**

Black Culture

Culture is a people's way of life. It includes a community's beliefs, language, art, music, dance, literature, religion, and stories. Black culture in North America is a blend of African and Western influences.

Many black writers learned storytelling and writing by listening to the stories told by their parents and grandparents. The first black writers struggled to make people aware of the evils of slavery and the unequal treatment of African North Americans. From the 1800s, African-American journals, such as the *North Star*, founded by freed slave Frederick Douglass, helped focus the fight for the abolition of slavery. The autobiographies of ex-slaves, which described first-hand the conditions of most black North Americans, convinced thousands that slavery was wrong.

After World War I (1914–1918), in the 1920s, Harlem in New York City became the black cultural center of North America. The age of new creativity is called the Harlem Renaissance. Young poets, artists, and novelists began to produce unique and powerful works that attracted wide attention. More books by African American authors were published in the '20s than ever before. Poets such as Langston Hughes became popular with both black and white readers. Novelists Zora Neale Hurston and Claude McKay won major awards. Plays by African American playwrights were performed on Broadway, and actors such as Paul Robeson became stars.

▲ A statue
the Canadi
sprinter Ho
Winston Je
in Vancouv
Stanley Pa
celebrates
achieveme
in sport.

Religion

In their homelands of West Africa, Africans followed different religions but often shared certain beliefs. Some Africans who were transported as slaves were Muslims. They followed the religion of Islam. Islam is based on the teachings of the prophet Muhammad who was born in Mecca, Saudi Arabia. Others worshipped the spirits of their ancestors and of the earth. In North America, white slave owners tried to prevent slaves from practicing their African religions. Some slave owners allowed slaves to practice Christianity, a religion that follows the teachings of Jesus Christ, who Christians believe is the son of God. Many slaves became Baptists and Methodists. Sometimes slaves were not allowed to attend white churches, so they formed their own, often in secret. The African Methodist Episcopal church was the first all-black Christian church in the United States. The British Methodist Episcopal church was the first all-black Christian church in Canada. These Christian churches became a refuge for African North Americans both before and after emancipation. They were places where dreams of freedom were **nurtured**. In the 1950s, many of the leaders of the civil rights movement were leaders of black churches. Today, churches are still an important part of many black communities. They are centers of music, worship, culture, and community support.

For a long time, black North Americans were rarely seen in films, and when they were, they were shown as field workers or maids. The few black actors working on movies faced discrimination. Hattie McDaniel, who won an Academy Award for her role in *Gone with the Wind*, was seated at the back of the hall during the ceremony.

In the 1970s, with African North Americans making up 40 per cent of the movie audience, things began to change. Films about African Americans were made, and actors such as James Earl Jones and Cicely Tyson became stars. African-American producers began making their own films.

Film producer and writer Spike Lee began his career in college. His first movie won a student Academy Award. Within four years, he wrote and directed an even more successful film which won the prize for best new film at the Cannes Film Festival in France. Over the years, Spike has continued to make movies that challenge ideas about black North America.

▼ **Phillis Wheatley (1753–1785) was a U.S. slave who became a poet.**

Customs and Traditions

Tradition has always been important to black North Americans. From the 1600s, African slaves brought their beliefs and customs to North America. Some have survived to become part of everyday life.

Music is one tradition that has survived hundreds of years of **oppression**. During the worst days of slavery, African North Americans sang. They sang about their pain, about their hopes for a better life, and their faith. They sang spirituals, ballads, and folk songs. They played the bonja, a musical instrument made from a hollow gourd, which their African ancestors had used for centuries.

Even after the end of slavery, African Americans had little chance to study music or take formal music lessons. They could not afford to buy expensive musical instruments, so they sang. Blues, with its sad melodies and hope for the end of injustice, began in the south after the Civil War. **Sharecroppers** sang songs of hardship while working in the fields. Blues music **evolved** from the "field holler" of slaves and music sung in black churches in the south. Ragtime, which also developed in the south after the Civil War, became the music of freedom, of a new life. Scott Joplin, the son of an ex-slave, was its most famous composer.

▲ In the 1920s and 1930s many black musicians played in very successful jazz bands.

▶ Music is an important part of black worship. Many popular singers got their start in gospel choirs.

28

Festivals and holidays

Today, African-American beliefs and traditions are celebrated in various holidays. The festival of Kwanzaa, based on traditional African harvest rituals, takes place over seven days in late December. Each day is dedicated to a guiding principle that helps strengthen the black community, including unity, faith, and purpose. Families light candles, discuss the seven principles, and celebrate black leaders. In the United States, Martin Luther King Jr. Day, held in January, honors the black leader who was killed in 1968. In both Canada and the United States, Black History Month, held in February, celebrates black culture and achievements. Caribana, a festival of Caribbean culture, is held every August in Toronto, Ontario. People come from all over Canada, the United States, and the West Indies to watch the Caribana parade with its colorfully costumed dancers. The festival has its roots in the celebrations of former slaves and their descendants in the Caribbean.

Blues music moved north from the cotton fields of Mississippi to Chicago in the early 1900s, as millions of black sharecroppers moved to the northern city to find work. Blues music developed into jazz, a blend of African rhythms and melodies with European styles. Jazz soon became one of the most popular forms of modern music. During the 1920s, Louis Armstrong and Jelly Roll Morton made records that made jazz known throughout the world. During the 1950s and 1960s, black musicians developed new styles of popular music, including rhythm-and-blues and rock 'n' roll. Artists, such as Smokey Robinson and Stevie Wonder, became famous through the black-owned Motown record label.

▼ The singer Lauryn Hill founded The Refugee Project which raises money for social programs for young people.

In the 1970s and 1980s, rap music, which began with street musicians reciting songs without backup music, emerged as a popular new style. Rap music has influenced both black and white culture in North America. Rap developed from hip hop culture which included breakdancing and graffiti art. Hip hop artists, such as Michael Franti of the group Spearhead, and Lauryn Hill, are also **social activists** who work to **empower** black people. Their music celebrates black history, culture, and traditions.

Here to Stay

Blacks in the United States and Canada have made important contributions to all aspects of their countries' society and culture. They feel pride in their accomplishments.

Between the 1970s and 1990s, African Americans, and the rapidly expanding African-Canadian community, made many new gains. Some were elected to high office at the provincial, state, or national level. For the first time, colleges and universities ran black studies programs that recognized the achievements of African North Americans. Black graduates excelled in business and as doctors, lawyers, scientists, and engineers. These young professionals swelled the ranks of the growing black middle class.

▲ Black activist Angela Davis was a major figure in 1970s black culture.

▼ Toronto's Caribana Festival celebrates Caribbean culture. Many immigrants from the Caribbean came to North America from the 1950s on. Caribana is one of the largest cultural festivals in North America.

Recent Achievements

African Americans and African Canadians have made many major contributions to North American life and culture. In 1989, Colin Powell was awarded the top U.S. military position, chairman of the Joint Chiefs of Staff. He was the youngest person and the first African American to hold the position. African-American **entrepreneurs** have built many large and successful companies. Berry Gordy, Jr. launched a small record company, Motown, which grew to be the largest independent record company in the world. George Elliott Clarke is an award-winning Canadian poet, playwright, and university professor. A descendant of Nova Scotia black Loyalists, he describes his writing as "bearing witness" to black life in Canada. Novelist Toni Morrison has written about black life in the United States in books such as *Beloved* and *Song of Solomon*. In 1993, she won the Nobel Prize for literature, one of the most important prizes awared to writers in the world.

▲ **Lillian Allen is a Jamaican-born Canadian dub poet whose works discuss racism. Dub poetry has its roots in a Caribbean culture and a type of music called reggae.**

Despite recent gains, blacks in North America still face many problems. Studies show that they are twice as likely to be unemployed as whites, and they may earn lower wages for similar work. One third of all black families live in poverty. They often receive poorer health care and have a shorter life expectancy than whites. Black people also sometimes suffer discrimination from the police and justice system.

In the last few decades, thousands of West Indian immigrants have left their homes in the Caribbean and moved to Canada and the United States, bringing their cultural traditions with them. Their arrival has changed the makeup of many black communities in North America. Refugees from war-torn African countries, such as Ethiopia and Somalia, have also built new homes in North America. Together with blacks who are the descendants of slaves who came here long ago, they are creating vibrant communities where many traditions of their homelands are being preserved.

▼ **Today, the contributions of blacks to all professions are being recognized.**

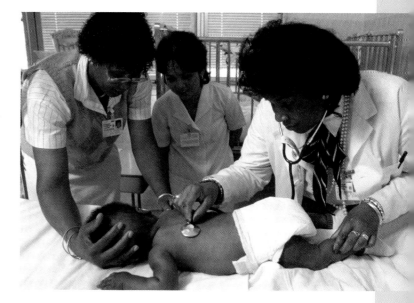

Glossary

abolitionist movement Group of people who worked towards the ending of slavery.

arson Setting fire to a property.

assassinate To murder by sudden or secret attack, usually from political or religious motives. The victim is usually an important person.

astronomer Someone who studies stars, planets, and moons.

boycott To refuse to use a service or buy certain goods.

brazier A metal basket in which coals are heated and held.

caravan Company of people traveling together.

cargo Goods carried in a truck, ship, or airplane.

colony Area of land settled or conquered by a distant state and controlled by it.

culture A group of people's way of life, including their language, beliefs and art.

curfew An order given to people to stay at home after a certain time in the evening.

discrimination To treat people unfairly because of their race, sex, or religion.

empire Group of countries ruled by one supreme authority.

empower To help someone become more powerful.

entrepreneur Business person.

evolve To change over time.

hold The inside part of a ship where goods are carried.

immigrant Someone who comes to settle in one country from another.

literacy Reading and writing.

Loyalist People supporting the British during the American Revolution.

mathematician Someone who works with numbers.

nurture To help to grow and develop.

oppression The cruel use of power, especially by governments.

plantation Estate on which cotton, tobacco, or tea is cultivated, and which requires slaves or cheap labor.

prejudice An unfair opinion.

prosperity Success and wealth.

profitable Something that makes money.

racism Belief that some races are better or worse than others.

reconstruction Rebuilding.

resist To fight against.

safe house Place where slaves could hide and organize secret activities.

scholar A wise person who studies a lot.

secede To withdraw from one group to form another, separate group.

segregated Separated according to race.

sharecropper A farmer who rents land from a landowner and can only keep a share of the harvest.

social activist Person who works in a public way to help other people.

Index

1 2 3 4 5 6 7 8 9 0 Printed in the USA 5 4 3 2 1 0